Hands-On History

American Revolution

by Michael Gravois

New York • Toronto • London • Auckland • Sydney
Mexico City • New Delhi • Hong Kong • Buenos Aires

SCHOLASTIC
Teaching
Resources

Dedication

To my dad, Warren Gravois,
for showing me America

Cover design by Jason Robinson
Interior design by Michael Gravois
Interior illustrations by Jim Palmer and Mona Mark

ISBN 0-439-07208-5

Table of Contents

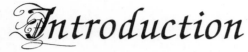

Introduction

As a middle-school teacher, I was always looking for ways to keep students interested and enthusiastic about learning. I developed activities and projects that helped me teach the required curriculum and also made my lessons fun, hands-on, diverse, and challenging.

I used an interactive-project approach with my fifth-grade students, and I can't stress enough how much they enjoyed it. Throughout each unit I had my students keep the activity sheets and projects in a pocket folder, so they could assemble a student-made textbook on the subject we were studying. They used these textbooks as a study guide for the final test. I was amazed at the higher-level thinking that took place in class discussions and by the degree of knowledge the students had acquired by the end of each unit. Parents even commented on the unique way the information was presented and how easy it was for their children to study for the final test. After seeing my students' success, I decided to put my ideas on paper. *Hands-On History: American Revolution* is a compilation of the activities I used to teach the American Revolution.

For each activity and project, I've included detailed instructions. Many of the activities incorporate language arts and critical thinking skills, such as differentiating fact and opinion, comparing and contrasting, the 5 Ws (who, what, where, when, why), understanding cause and effect, writing a letter, brainstorming, and sequencing.

I hope your students enjoy these projects as much as mine did.

How to Use This Book

Supplies

At the beginning of the school year, ask students to bring in the materials needed to create projects throughout the year. Also arrange the classroom desks into clusters, each with a bin to hold pens, markers, glue sticks, scissors, and other needed supplies. This enables students to share the materials. You should have each of your students bring in the following supplies:

- a roll of tape
- several glue sticks
- a good pair of scissors
- a packet of colored pencils
- a packet of thin, colored markers
- a project folder (pocket-type) to hold papers and other materials related to the projects

Maximizing Learning

Because students have different learning styles, you may want to first orally summarize the information you will be covering that day. Then you can read the related section in the textbook or trade book. Finally, have students complete the activity. This not only exposes visual, aural, and artistic learners to the information through their strongest learning style, but it also allows all students to review the same information several times.

Beginning the Unit

THE DOMINO EFFECT: CAUSES OF THE AMERICAN REVOLUTION

History provides a wonderful opportunity to teach cause and effect, and nowhere in U.S. history is cause and effect more readily apparent than during the Revolutionary War period. In a perfect illustration of the domino effect, a clear series of events led to other events that ultimately resulted in war.

To begin this unit discuss the domino effect with your class, having previously set up a trail of dominoes which ends at a house of cards or other unstable structure. Explain that when one domino falls over (the cause) it results in another domino falling over (the effect). The "effect" of each domino falling becomes, in turn, the "cause" of another domino falling. Explain that the toppling of the house of cards is the final effect of the domino trail. Push over the first domino and watch the fun. This never ceases to get the students' attention—the more elaborate the trail, the more enthusiastic the students become.

As students proceed through the unit, relate each activity to the previous one in order to show the cause-and-effect progression that led up to the American Revolution.

Cause-and-Effect Title Page

Materials: copies of page 27, scissors, glue sticks, copier paper, oaktag (optional)

1. Pass out one copy of the template on page 27 to each student.
2. Have students cut out the burst and the 12 dominoes along the dotted lines.
3. Then have them fold the flap at the bottom of each domino and glue it to another piece of paper, arranging the dominoes in a line that snakes across the page (as shown to the right). Oaktag will make this page more durable.
4. Students should write "The American Revolution" on the burst and glue it on the paper after the twelfth domino. As you study each of the twelve events leading up to the war, the students will lift the corresponding domino and write the event underneath it. The students can store this sheet in their project folders while studying this unit, and it can become the title page of their interactive study guide at the end of the unit.

American Revolution Bulletin Board

Materials: green and brown construction paper, copies of page 28, scissors

At the beginning of the American Revolution unit, set up a bulletin board that students will add to as the unit unfolds. First, cover the bulletin board with green paper to look like grass. Next, use brown and green paper to make trees, which you can add to the right half of the board. Then, add the title "Revolutionary Vocabulary" across the top.

Students should take turns writing vocabulary words and definitions on a "soldier" cut out from the template on page 28. They may color the soldiers if they wish. Add the British soldiers to the left half so they are marching in line. Add the American soldiers to the right half so they are crouching behind trees. Not only do students learn the relevant vocabulary, but they also learn about the different fighting styles of the two armies. These different fighting styles helped America win the war.

Keep a supply of "vocabulary soldiers" handy for student use as new words come up in class. See the word list below for some suggestions.

Suggested Vocabulary Words

allies: people who unite with others for a special purpose, especially in war

boycott: to refuse to do business with or buy goods from another person or country

Committees of Correspondence: committees formed by the colonies to quickly inform colonists about important political events

delegate: a representative

Loyalist: an American colonist who supported Great Britain and was loyal to King George III during the American Revolution

militia: a group of volunteers that fought in a part-time army during the American Revolution

minuteman: a colonist who would be ready to fight the British at a minute's notice

Patriot: an American colonist who supported the fight for independence

rebel: to resist the authority of one's government

repeal: to cancel a law

republic: a form of government in which the citizens elect representatives to run the country

traitor: someone who betrays his or her country

treaty: an agreement made by negotiation, especially between two states or governments

French and Indian War Lockbook

Materials: copies of pages 29–31, scissors, markers

Have students write "French and Indian War" under the first domino of their Cause-and-Effect Title Page.

Students will create a lockbook of the French and Indian War. They will learn how the geography of America changed as a result of this war, and they will learn the who, what, when, where, why, and how of this war.

CREATING THE LOCKBOOK

1. Copy the templates from pages 29 and 30 back to back so that panel 8 is directly opposite panel 7.
2. Cut the template on page 31 in half, and copy the halves back to back so that panel 3 is opposite panel 4.
3. Distribute copies to students and have them cut the first page along the dashed line. Have them cut off the blank half of the second page. (Each student should have three half-sheets containing a total of 12 panels.)
4. Then have students select the page marked "cover" and cut along the dotted line so that there is a hole in the center of the page (figure 1).
5. The other two pages should be cut from the edges along the dotted lines, as shown (figure 2).
6. Have students hold the page with the hole so that panels 2 and 7 are facing them. Then have them curl or fold the top and bottom of panel 10 and feed it through the center hole between panels 2 and 7, as shown (figure 3). Ask them to open up the curled page so it "locks" into place. Then have students repeat this step by curling the back cover panel and sliding it through the hole between panels 2 and 5.
7. Finally, ask students to fold the lockbook pages making sure that the pages are in the proper order. On the cover they may use creative lettering to name the book. (Remind them that the topic is the French and Indian War.) Students can also add an illustration under the title.

figure 1

figure 2

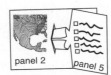

figure 3

FINISHING THE LOCKBOOK

Panels 2 and 3

The map on panel 2 shows the land of North America in 1750 and the countries that claimed it. Have students fill in the squares of the key on panel 3 so they correspond with the sections of the map on panel 2. Students should use the following patterns:

 British: dots

French: circles

Spanish: stripes

Disputed or unclaimed by Europeans: crosshatching

You might have students color code the key and map as an extension activity. For example, students could color all the land claimed by the British red, and then they could color in the corresponding box on the key.

Panels 4 and 5

The map on panel 4 shows the land of North America after the French and Indian War in 1763. Students should use the same patterns to fill in the key on panel 5 as they did for the key on panel 3. The additional square should be colored as follows:

 Russian: black

Panels 6 through 11

Explain to students that every good article answers the 5 Ws and How. Tell them that they will answer six questions about the French and Indian War on the six remaining panels. Allow them to use their textbook to answer the questions.

Suggested Answers for Lockbooks

Panel 6:
The French and Indians fought against the British and American colonists.

Panel 7:
The war occurred between 1754 and 1763.

Panel 8:
The two sides were fighting for control of North America.

Panel 9:
The war was fought in North America.

Panel 10:
France lost the war.

Panel 11:
Britain gained control of all land east of the Mississippi River as well as all of New France.

Review the answers to the questions with your class to make sure everyone has the correct answers. Students can then put the lockbooks in their project folders.

The Proclamation of 1763

Materials: white or tan construction paper

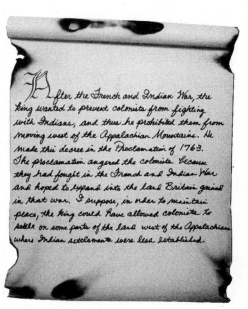

Have students write "The Proclamation of 1763" under the second domino of their Cause-and-Effect Title Page.

Be sure to explain how the events the students will study in this unit are both causes and effects. Each event they'll learn about happened as a result of the previous event. For instance, the Proclamation of 1763 was ordered as a result of the French and Indian War. The American colonists wanted to move farther west, but that would have meant further fighting with the Indians, which King George III wanted to avoid. This proclamation prohibited colonists from moving west of the Appalachian Mountains, and preserved this land as hunting grounds for the American Indians.

CREATING THE PROCLAMATION

1. Give each student a sheet of white or tan construction paper. Ask students to place the paper in front of them vertically.
2. In the center of this paper, students should write a complete, detailed paragraph that answers the three questions below. (Suggested answers follow each question.)
3. Ask them to curl the top and bottom edges toward the center to make it look like a scroll.
4. Display the proclamations on a bulletin board under a banner that reads "Hear Ye! Hear Ye!"

Suggested Answers for Proclamations

1. **Why did King George III issue the Proclamation of 1763?**

   After the French and Indian War, the king wanted to prevent colonists from fighting with Indians, and thus he prohibited them from moving west of the Appalachian Mountains.

2. **Why did the proclamation anger the colonists?**

   The proclamation angered the colonists because they had fought in the French and Indian War and hoped to expand into the land Britain gained in that war.

3. **Can you think of a compromise that might have satisfied both the king and the colonists?**

   The king could have allowed colonists to settle on some parts of the land west of the Appalachians where Indian settlements were less established.

Q-and-A Flip Book About Taxes

Materials: copies of page 32, scissors, construction paper, colored pencils or markers, *America Rock* video (©1995, American Broadcasting Companies)

 Have students write "Unfair Taxes" under the third domino of their Cause-and-Effect Title Page.

The first song from the Schoolhouse Rock video *America Rock* is a catchy song called "No More Kings." Start the next three lessons with this video. By the end of the third viewing, the class will be singing along.

Students can make this flip book after they have read about and discussed the ways Britain unfairly taxed the American colonists. It is a fun way for them to summarize and apply the information.

CREATING THE FLIP BOOK

1. Pass out copies of page 32 and have students cut out the box of questions.
2. Next have them cut along the dotted lines (stopping at the vertical gray strip) to create five horizontal strips.
3. Then have students glue the left side of the strips onto a sheet of construction paper.
4. Now have them write a title across the top of the page and write the answer to each question under its strip.

Suggested Answers for Flip Books

1. **Why did Great Britain need to raise money?**

   Great Britain borrowed a great deal of money to pay for the French and Indian War. It was necessary to pay this money back, so Britain taxed the colonists to raise money.

2. **What was the Sugar Act?**

   The Sugar Act placed a tax on sugar and molasses.

3. **How did Great Britain enforce the payment of taxes?**

   Because the colonists sometimes smuggled goods into the colonies to avoid paying taxes, Great Britain sent officials to America to search people's homes and businesses.

4. **What was the Stamp Act? What things were taxed under this act?**

   The Stamp Act required that colonists pay a tax when they bought certain items, such as newspapers, calendars, and playing cards. The items were marked with a stamp to show the tax had been paid.

5. **Who were the Sons of Liberty? What did they do?**

   The Sons of Liberty were groups of colonists that protested against the British and even attacked British tax agents.

★ ★ ★ ★ ★ ★ ★ ★ ★ ★ ★ ★ ★ ★ ★ ★

Boston Massacre Time Line Flag

Materials: copies of page 33, colored pencils or markers

Have students write "Boston Massacre" under the fourth domino of their Cause-and-Effect Title Page.

Explain to students that there are certain "clue words" that indicate the order in which things occur. Four of the most common sequence words are *first, next, then,* and *finally.* Write these four words on the board in a column. Ask students to tell you the sequence of events of the Boston Massacre leading up to the death of five colonists. For example: First, Great Britain sent troops to the colonies to make sure the colonists paid taxes. This angered the colonists. Next, a crowd of angry colonists in Boston gathered around one lone British soldier and jeered at him. They threw snowballs with rocks in them. Then, more British soldiers arrived and the crowd grew larger. Finally, someone yelled "Fire!" and the soldiers shot their guns. Five colonists were killed.

CREATING THE TIME LINE FLAG

1. First, pass out copies of the template on page 33.
2. Next, have students write the words *First, Next, Then,* and *Finally* in the four flags, from top to bottom.
3. Then, ask them to write the sequence of events that led up to the Boston Massacre next to the appropriate flag. Encourage them to list the four events they consider most significant.
4. Finally, let students color and decorate their flags.

A Gravestone for Crispus Attucks

Materials: copies of page 34, scissors, glue sticks, colored pencils or markers, copier paper

CREATING THE GRAVESTONE AND EPITAPH FOR CRISPUS ATTUCKS

1. Pass out copies of the template on page 34, and have students cut around the gravestone only along the dotted line, leaving the left side attached.
2. Ask students to glue the paper surrounding the gravestone to another piece of paper, leaving the gravestone itself unglued. The gravestone becomes a door which opens, revealing the blank page behind it.
3. Have students design a gravestone for Crispus Attucks. Tell students that his year of birth was probably 1723 and his year of death was 1770.
4. On the paper behind the gravestone, have students write an obituary for Crispus Attucks. They should include a description of who he was and what his role was in the Boston Massacre. Remind students to use complete sentences as they write the obituary.

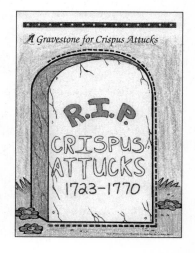

11

Boston Tea Party Step Book

Materials: copier paper or construction paper, scissors, markers or colored pencils

 Have students write "The Tea Act" under the fifth domino, "The Boston Tea Party" under the sixth domino, and "The Intolerable Acts" under the seventh domino of their Cause-and-Effect Title Page.

Explain to students that the series of events they will be studying next is a clear example of cause and effect. Students will create a step book to record information about these three events.

CREATING THE STEP BOOK

1. Give each student a sheet of white paper or construction paper.
2. Have them cut the paper in half widthwise, as shown.
3. Ask students to place the pages on top of each other so that approximately ³/₄" of the bottom page is showing below the top page.
4. Next they should fold the pages backwards so they wrap around, exposing two more ³/₄" strips at the bottom. Instruct students to crease the top fold and staple it.
5. Have students create a title and illustration for their step book on the cover. Remind them that the subject of this project is the Boston Tea Party.
6. Then have them write *Cause*, *Effect*, and *Repercussion* on the three exposed strips of the lower panels (see the example below).

FINISHING THE STEP BOOK

1. Students should open the step book to the first page (labeled "cause"). Have students use creative lettering to write "The Tea Act" on the top half. They should draw a symbol that represents the event, such as a tea cup or tea bag, and then write a complete paragraph about the Tea Act on the bottom half. (Suggested answers for the step books appear on page 13.)
2. Have students lift the next flap, revealing the "effect" page. Have them write "Boston Tea Party" on the top half and illustrate this famous event. Then have them write a paragraph describing this event on the bottom half.
3. Have students lift the last flap, revealing the "repercussion" page. Then have them write "The Intolerable Acts" in creative script and illustrate this (for example, a "Closed" sign on Boston Harbor). On the bottom half, they should write a complete paragraph describing the Intolerable Acts and how the colonists reacted to them.

Suggested Answers for Step Books

Cause: Although the British repealed most of the taxes on the colonists, the Tea Act kept the tax on tea in place. This act also gave one British company control of all the tea trade, threatening the business of American tea merchants.

Effect: In 1773, a group of colonists, angered by the Tea Act, disguised themselves as Indians and boarded a British ship in Boston Harbor. They dumped 343 crates of valuable tea into the harbor.

Repercussion: In response to the Boston Tea Party, the British closed Boston Harbor and forced colonists to house and feed British soldiers. The colonists called these the "Intolerable Acts."

Now-and-Then Contrast Book of the First Continental Congress

Materials: copies of page 35, scissors, glue sticks, construction paper

Have students write "The First Continental Congress" under the eighth domino of their Cause-and-Effect Title Page.

Help students better understand the importance of the First Continental Congress by having them examine world events today. Ask students to research current boycotts and sanctions against other countries and contrast them with the boycotts that occurred as a result of the First Continental Congress.

CREATING THE NOW-AND-THEN CONTRAST BOOKS

1. Pass out a copy of the template on page 35 and a sheet of construction paper to each student.
2. Have students cut the template in half along the vertical dotted line.
3. Ask them to fold the two sheets of paper in half along the dashed line so that the words "Then" and "Now" appear on the cover of each.
4. Students should glue the back of each sheet to the piece of construction paper. (The "Then" sheet should be on the left.)
5. Tell students to use creative lettering to write the title "The First Continental Congress" under the word "Then." Have them lift the flap and write a complete paragraph describing the 5 Ws of this event.
6. Have students write a title under the word "Now" that describes a current world situation involving the use of tactics similar to those used by the First Continental Congress. Under that flap, have them write a paragraph that focuses on the 5 Ws of this event.
7. Students can write a title such as "Boycotts Then and Now" across the top of the page.

Mini-Book of Paul Revere's Ride

Materials: copies of page 36, scissors, colored markers or pencils

Have students write "Paul Revere's Ride to Lexington and Concord" under the ninth domino of their Cause-and-Effect Title Page.

Before doing this activity, read and discuss the poem "Paul Revere's Ride" by Henry Wadsworth Longfellow. There are many beautifully illustrated picture books of this poem available in libraries.

Provide students with copies of the template on page 36. Read the following directions aloud to the class. Wait for all students to complete each step before moving on to the next one.

CREATING THE MINI-BOOK

1. Fold the template in half, as shown.

2. Fold it in half again in the same direction.

3. Fold this long, narrow strip in half in the opposite direction.

4. Open up the paper to the Step 2 position, and cut halfway down the vertical fold.

5. Open the paper up and turn it horizontally. There should be a hole in the center where you made the cut.

6. Fold the paper in half lengthwise so the writing is on the outside.

7. Push in on the ends of the paper so the slit opens up. Push until the center panels meet.

8. Fold the four pages into a mini-book. Flip through the pages so that the cover is on the outside. Crease the binding.

Have students illustrate each page of their mini-book, providing a picture to go with Longfellow's words. The drawings should be colorful and fill each frame. Students can add a small illustration to the cover as well. As part of their final test on the American Revolution, consider having students memorize these lines from Longfellow's poem. Memorization is a useful skill for students to develop, and this also exposes them to poetry recitation.

Puzzle-Piece Time Line of Lexington and Concord

Materials: copies of page 37, scissors, colored markers or pencils, tape

The Battle of Lexington and Concord marked the start of the American Revolution with "the shot heard round the world." Invite students to learn more about this historical period by having them create a puzzle-piece time line that sequences important events related to this famous battle.

CREATING THE PUZZLE-PIECE TIME LINE

1. Ask students to research the Battle of Lexington and Concord. Allow them to use textbooks, trade books, Internet search engines, and encyclopedias.
2. As they conduct their research, instruct students to write a list of key events associated with this battle: the organization of the minutemen, Paul Revere's ride, the shot heard round the world, the march to Concord, the British retreat, and so on. In note form, students should write the date of the events and a sentence describing each one.
3. Then ask students to choose five important events from their list. Give them five copies of the Puzzle-Piece Template. Have students complete a puzzle piece for each of the five events, following the directions at the top of the template page.
4. After they have completed the puzzle pieces, students should cut them out and tape them, from behind, into a long strip.
5. Display the time lines on a bulletin board for everyone to see.

April 18, 1775
British troops leave Boston to arrest colonial leaders.

April 18, 1775
Paul Revere and William Dawes alert the minutemen that the Redcoats are coming.

April 19, 1775
Minutemen and British troops meet at Lexington, where a shot from a stray British gun leads to more British firing.

A Letter From the Second Continental Congress

Materials: copies of page 38, small envelopes, colored markers or pencils

Have students write "The Second Continental Congress" under the tenth domino of their Cause-and-Effect Title Page.

Before starting the activity, you may wish to review with students the proper form for writing a business letter and addressing the envelope. Refer students to a language arts textbook for examples. This activity can serve as a homework assignment or it can be done during class time.

CREATING THE LETTER AND ENVELOPE

1. Give each student a small envelope and a copy of the graphic organizer on page 38.
2. Explain to students that they will be writing a business letter from John Adams to George Washington, urging him to accept the nomination as Commander-in-Chief of the Continental Army. Even though Washington was in attendance at the Second Continental Congress, have students pretend the letter was sent to his home in Mount Vernon, Virginia.

3. Discuss with students the importance of point of view in a letter, and how Adams might persuade Washington to take the job.
4. Describe the significance of a postmark and how it is used to cancel stamps. You may wish to pass around some canceled letters so that students can see what a postmark looks like. Remind students that this letter was mailed from Philadelphia after the Second Continental Congress began on May 10, 1775.
5. After students write the letters and address the envelopes, they should design a stamp related to an event in American history that pre-dates the Second Continental Congress and draw it on the envelope.

The letter and envelope can be stored in the students' project folders until they are ready to construct their interactive textbooks at the end of the unit.

Guide Book to Bunker Hill

Materials: copies of pages 39 and 40 photocopied back to back

Have students write "The Battle of Bunker Hill" under the eleventh domino of their Cause-and-Effect Title Page.

CREATING THE GUIDE BOOK

1. Copy the templates from pages 39 and 40 back to back so that panel 1 is opposite panel 3, and pass them out to students.
2. Have students follow the directions on panel 6 to complete their guide books. The guides will help them improve their graph-reading skills and organize their thoughts for writing a short essay.
3. Students can create a cover for their guide book first, with a title and an illustration related to the Battle of Bunker Hill.
4. Next they should use the graph on panel 3 to answer the questions on panel 2. They may need scratch paper to do the math.
5. Finally, they should write a short essay on panels 4 and 5 that answers the questions listed on panel 6.

Suggested Answers for Guide Books

Graph Answers:

1. about 5,400
2. about 1,000
3. about 400
4. about 1,100
5. about 50%
6. about 2,800

Essay Answers:

1. Bunker Hill overlooked Boston. Cannons could be fired from the hill onto the city.

2. Three battles were fought. The American militia overpowered the British in the first two battles, but during the third they ran out of ammunition and had to retreat.

3. The general gave this order so that the soldiers would conserve their ammunition. He wanted every shot to count.

4. The Battle of Bunker Hill boosted the confidence of the colonists by showing that they were able to hold their own against the British troops.

Declaration of Independence Quiz Panels

Materials: copies of pages 41 and 42, scissors, glue sticks, copier paper or light-colored construction paper, *America Rock* video (©1995, American Broadcasting Companies)

Have students write "The Declaration of Independence" under the twelfth domino of their Cause-and-Effect Title Page.

Before beginning this activity, you may wish to watch "Fireworks" from the Schoolhouse Rock video *America Rock*, which features a catchy song and cartoon about the Declaration of Independence.

CREATING THE QUIZ PANELS

1. Pass out copies of pages 41 and 42 and two sheets of blank paper to each student.
2. Ask students to cut out the large outer box on each of the templates.
3. Next have them poke a hole in the center dot on each page with the sharp point of their scissors and cut along the solid lines.
4. Then have them fold the panels along the dotted lines.
5. Instruct students to glue the perimeter of each box onto a piece of white paper or light-colored construction paper. The students should be able to lift up the flaps in order to answer the questions on the paper behind each panel.
6. Have students work individually or in pairs to answer the questions.

Suggested Answers for Quiz Panels

1. Thomas Jefferson
2. July 4, 1776
3. John Hancock; so the king could read his name without wearing his spectacles.
4. life, liberty, and the pursuit of happiness
5. He meant that all the colonies had to join together against Britain, or else each member of the Congress would be hanged for treason.
6. In a democratic republic the people have the power and they elect government officials. In the British government, the king had most of the power.

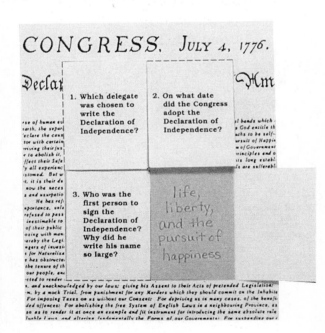

Military Matchbooks

Materials: copies of page 43, scissors, colored pencils

All of the events studied thus far led up to the fateful event that would change America forever: the American Revolution. Have students write "The American Revolution" in the burst after the last domino of their Cause-and-Effect Title Page.

Have students construct military matchbooks in order to help them understand the advantages and disadvantages held by the American and British armies.

CREATING THE MILITARY MATCHBOOKS

1. Give each student a copy of the template on page 43.
2. Have them cut the template horizontally along the two dashed lines.
3. Next have students place the two matchbooks in front of them—with the writing faceup—and fold the bottom strip up along the bottom line and crease it.
4. Then ask students to fold the top panel down, tucking it under the lower strip so it closes like a matchbook.
5. On the cover of one matchbook, have students use creative lettering to write the title "Military Advantages" and draw a simple icon related to one of the armies' advantages.
6. On the other matchbook, instruct students to write "Military Disadvantages" and draw a simple icon related to one of the armies' disadvantages.
7. On both of the lower strips, have them write "Americans and British."
8. On the board draw the Advantages/Disadvantages charts that are inside the two matchbooks (see the example to the right). Ask students for their opinions about what they think were the advantages and disadvantages of each of the armies. As you write the answers on the board, students should write them in their matchbooks. (Suggested answers appear on page 20.)

Military Advantages	
A M E R I C A N S	
B R I T I S H	

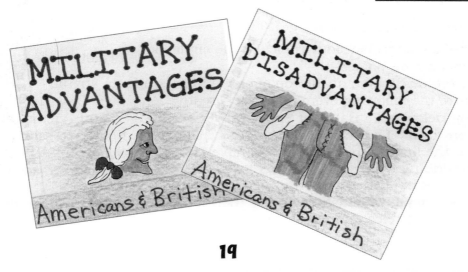

Mini-Book of Revolutionary Heroes

Materials: 11" x 17" copier or construction paper, colored pencils or markers, scissors

CREATING THE MINI-BOOK

1. Give each student a sheet of paper.
2. Read aloud the directions for creating mini-books on page 14.
3. Have students give the book a title. Have them write "_____'s (Student's Name) Mini-Book of Revolutionary Heroes" and draw a related picture.
4. Divide the class into groups of five. Have each student in the group research one hero. (See the suggested list below.)
5. After researching their hero, students might meet with you to review the information they have collected.
6. Have students join their groups and share what they've learned.
7. As information is shared, group members should record the data about each hero on one page of the mini-book. They should include a title with the hero's name and a small illustration.
8. On the sixth page, have students create an entry titled "Benedict Arnold: America's Most Famous Traitor." You may wish to assign this topic to one student or research Benedict Arnold together as a class.

Revolutionary Heroes

Abigail Adams
John Adams
Samuel Adams
Ethan Allen
Nathan Hale
Alexander Hamilton
Mary Ludwig Hays (Molly Pitcher)
Patrick Henry
John Paul Jones
Thomas Paine
Deborah Sampson
Friedrich von Steuben
Phyllis Wheatly

Readers Theater: The Boston Tea Party

Materials: copies of *The Boston Tea Party* (pages 45–48)

Reading plays aloud can provide students with opportunities to make connections between history and their own lives. Taking on a role, even for a short time, allows learners to become part of the story of our history, to become emotionally involved in the stories of other people, and to explore choices and lives foreign from their own.

Give each student a copy of the play *The Boston Tea Party* by Sarah J. Glasscock, assign parts, and have students read it aloud. Consider having students perform the play for other classes or having them turn it into a radio play, complete with sound effects and music.

After the class reads the play, you may wish to use the following activities to extend students' understanding of the Boston Tea Party and the American Revolution in general.

No Tea for Me!

Divide the class into two groups: the British and the colonists. Hold discussions about the Tea Tax. Were the groups able to find a compromise? Would they have been able to prevent the Boston Tea Party? If so, how would that have changed the course of American history?

Right or Wrong?

Bostonians took matters into their own hands. Men trespassed on British ships and dumped the cargo. Women forced a merchant to open his warehouse and then took his coffee. Ask students to consider why we consider these people heroic rather than criminal. Is it ever right to break the law?

I Protest!

Ask students to imagine they are shop owners in 1773 Boston, and tea is their best-selling product. Then the Tea Act is passed and the British refuse to give them a license to sell tea. What would they do? Encourage students to make their voices heard in England through an editorial or a political cartoon, a letter to King George III, a pamphlet, or even a poem or song.

American Revolution
Study Guide

Create a wonderful study guide for students by having them compile all of their mini-books, activities, and projects into an interactive American Revolution "textbook." Over the course of the unit, ask students to save all of their papers and projects in a pocket folder. At the end of the unit, use a binding machine to put them all together. If you don't have access to one, use a three-hole punch and yarn. On the next three pages you'll find suggestions for compiling each page.

Materials: all of the projects students have created, 8½" x 11" paper, binding machine (if available) or hole punch with yarn

COVER

When binding the textbooks, add a page of heavy stock to the front and back. Students can use creative lettering to add a title, and then draw a total of ten icons on the front and back covers. The icons can represent any ten things the student learned over the course of the unit. Have students number the icons, and then, on the inside front cover, write a complete sentence describing the significance of each icon.

PAGE 1

Include the CAUSE-AND-EFFECT TITLE PAGE as page 1.

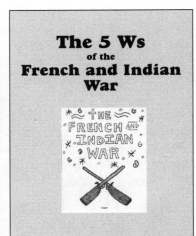

PAGE 2

Students can glue their FRENCH AND INDIAN WAR LOCKBOOK onto a sheet of paper, which can be bound in as page 2. Encourage them to add a title and decorate the page.

PAGE 3

Uncurl the ends of the PROCLAMATION OF 1763 and bind it into the textbook for page 3.

A FLIP BOOK ABOUT TAXES ON THE COLONIES

1. Why did Great Britain need to raise money?

The Sugar Act placed a tax on sugar and molasses.

2. How did Great Britain enforce the payment of taxes?

3. What was the Stamp Act? What kinds of things did it tax?

4. Who were the Sons of Liberty? What did they do?

PAGE 4

The Q-AND-A FLIPBOOK ABOUT TAXES becomes page 4 of the interactive textbook.

PAGE 5

Use the BOSTON MASSACRE TIME LINE FLAG as page 5.

Boston Massacre Time Line Flag

FIRST Great Britain sent troops to the colonies to make sure they paid taxes. This angered the colonists.

NEXT A crowd of angry colonists in Boston jeered at a lone British soldier. They threw snowballs with rocks in them.

THEN More British soldiers arrived and the crowd grew larger.

A Gravestone for Crispus Attucks

R.I.P.
CRISPUS
ATTUCKS
1723–1770

PAGE 6

Include the GRAVESTONE FOR CRISPUS ATTUCKS as page 6.

PAGE 7

Students can glue their BOSTON TEA PARTY STEP BOOK onto a sheet of paper, which can be used for page 7.

One thing always leads to another!

GINA'S STEP BOOK OF The Boston Tea Party

CAUSE
EFFECT
REPERCUSSION

PAGE 8

Students can glue the backs of their Now-AND-THEN CONTRAST BOOK OF THE FIRST CONTINENTAL CONGRESS to a sheet of paper, which can be used as page 8.

Now BUY AMERICAN OIL

Then THE FIRST CONTINENTAL CONGRESS

BOYCOTTS THEN & Now

PAGE 9

Students can create a pocket-page to hold their MINI-BOOK OF PAUL REVERE'S RIDE by folding a piece of 8½" x 11" paper in half horizontally, slipping another sheet of paper into the fold, and taping the sides. Encourage students to add a title and decorate the page.

Paul Revere's Ride
by Henry Wadsworth Longfellow

Look inside children, and you shall find here my mini-book of Paul Revere!

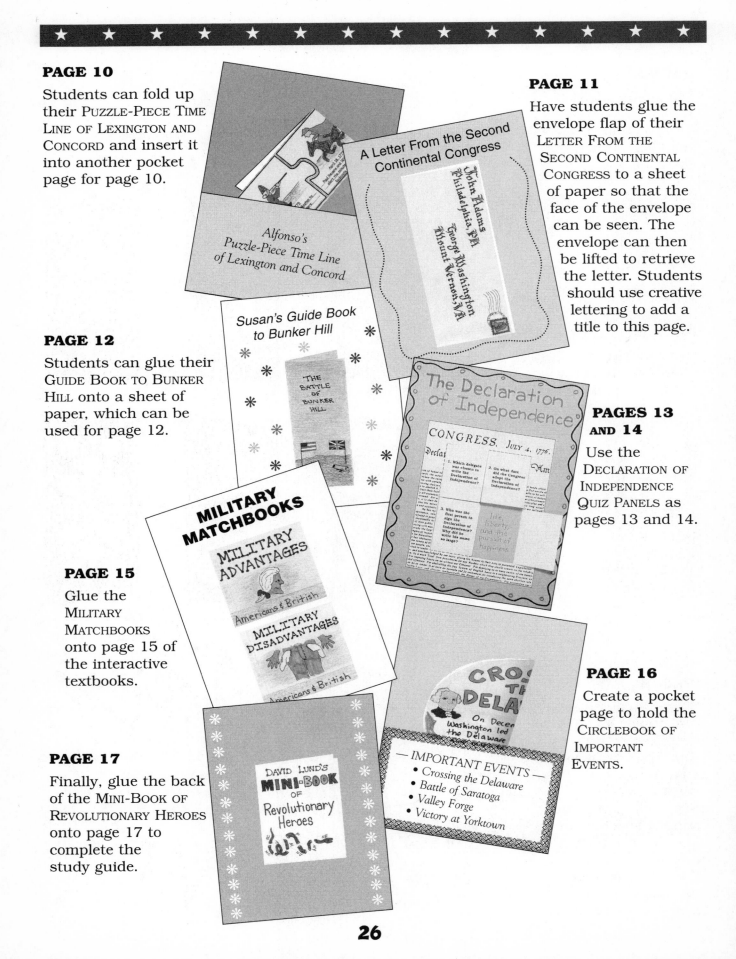

PAGE 10

Students can fold up their PUZZLE-PIECE TIME LINE OF LEXINGTON AND CONCORD and insert it into another pocket page for page 10.

Alfonso's
Puzzle-Piece Time Line
of Lexington and Concord

A Letter From the Second Continental Congress

John Adams
Philadelphia, PA

George Washington
Mount Vernon, VA

PAGE 11

Have students glue the envelope flap of their LETTER FROM THE SECOND CONTINENTAL CONGRESS to a sheet of paper so that the face of the envelope can be seen. The envelope can then be lifted to retrieve the letter. Students should use creative lettering to add a title to this page.

Susan's Guide Book
to Bunker Hill

THE
BATTLE
OF
BUNKER
HILL

PAGE 12

Students can glue their GUIDE BOOK TO BUNKER HILL onto a sheet of paper, which can be used for page 12.

The Declaration of Independence

CONGRESS. JULY 4. 1776.

1. Which delegate was chosen to write the Declaration of Independence?

2. On what date did the Congress adopt the Declaration of Independence?

3. Who was the first person to sign the Declaration of Independence? Why did he write his name so large?

life, liberty, and the pursuit of happiness

PAGES 13 AND 14

Use the DECLARATION OF INDEPENDENCE QUIZ PANELS as pages 13 and 14.

MILITARY MATCHBOOKS

MILITARY
ADVANTAGES

Americans & British

MILITARY
DISADVANTAGES

Americans & British

PAGE 15

Glue the MILITARY MATCHBOOKS onto page 15 of the interactive textbooks.

CROS
TH
DELA

On Decem
Washington led
the Delaware

— IMPORTANT EVENTS —
• Crossing the Delaware
• Battle of Saratoga
• Valley Forge
• Victory at Yorktown

PAGE 16

Create a pocket page to hold the CIRCLEBOOK OF IMPORTANT EVENTS.

DAVID LUND'S
MINI-BOOK
OF
Revolutionary
Heroes

PAGE 17

Finally, glue the back of the MINI-BOOK OF REVOLUTIONARY HEROES onto page 17 to complete the study guide.

The Domino Effect: Causes of the American Revolution

Vocabulary Soldiers

word:

_____

definition:

_____

_____

_____

_____

word:

_____

definition:

_____

_____

_____

_____

Why did the war take place?

Cover

What were the results of the war?

Hands-On History: American Revolution Scholastic Teaching Resources, page 29

☐— **BRITISH**

As a result of the war, France gave all of its land east of the Mississippi River, plus all of New France, to Great Britain.

☐— **FRENCH**

This small part of America was the only land held by France after the war.

☐— **SPANISH**

France had given all of its land west of the Mississippi River to Spain as a reward for Spain's help during the war.

☐— **DISPUTED OR UNCLAIMED BY EUROPEANS**

☐— **RUSSIAN**

⋯⋰— **Proclamation line of 1763**

North America in 1750

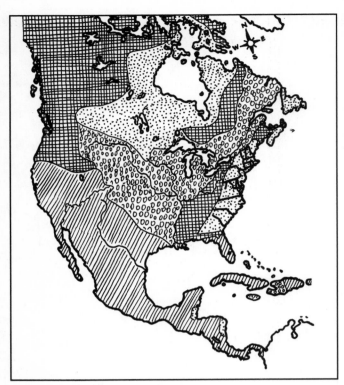

Panel 2

Who?

Who fought in the French and Indian War?

Panel 6

Where?

Where did the war take place?

Panel 9

North America in 1763

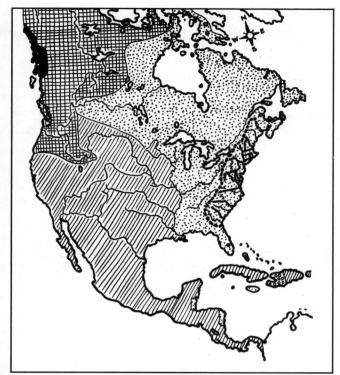

Panel 4

Hands-On History: American Revolution Scholastic Teaching Resources, page 31

How?

How did the map of North America change after the war?

Panel 11

Key

☐ — **BRITISH**

☐ — **FRENCH**

☐ — **SPANISH**

☐ — **DISPUTED OR UNCLAIMED BY EUROPEANS**

Panel 3

Q-and-A Flip Book About Taxes

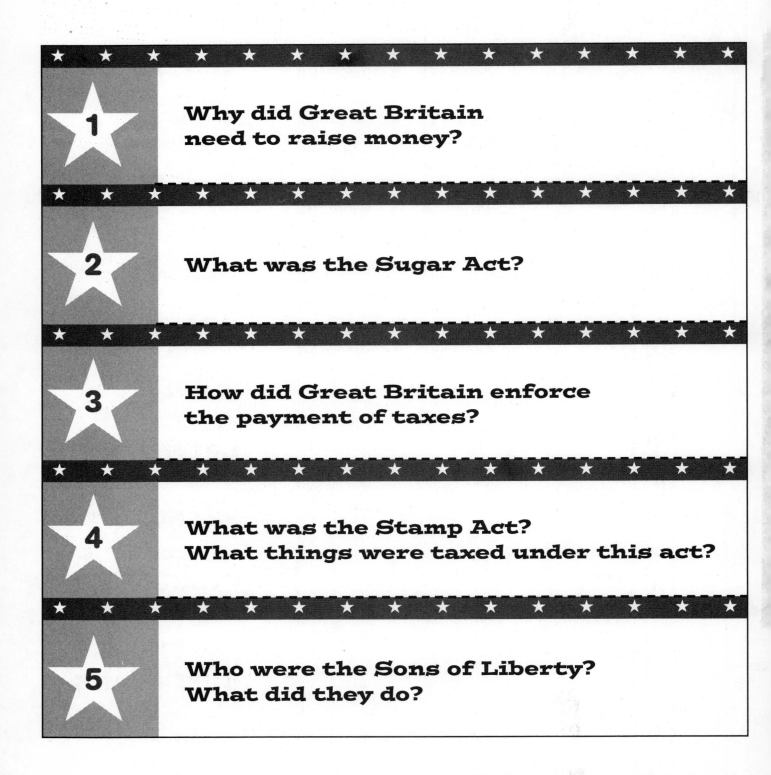

1 Why did Great Britain
need to raise money?

2 What was the Sugar Act?

3 How did Great Britain enforce
the payment of taxes?

4 What was the Stamp Act?
What things were taxed under this act?

5 Who were the Sons of Liberty?
What did they do?

Boston Massacre Time Line Flag

A Gravestone for Crispus Attucks

Cut along this line.

Fold along this line.

Fold along this line.

One, if by land, and two, if by sea;
And I on the opposite shore will be,

Ready to ride and spread the alarm
Through every Middlesex village and farm,

He said to his friend, "If the British march
By land or sea from the town tonight,
Hang a lantern aloft in the belfry arch
of the North Church tower as a signal light.

For the country folk to be up and to arm."

On the eighteenth of April, in Seventy-five;
Hardly a man is now alive
Who remembers that famous day and year.

Back Cover

Listen my children, and you shall hear
Of the midnight ride of Paul Revere.

by Henry Wadsworth Longfellow

Paul Revere's Ride

Puzzle-Piece Template

1. Print the date of the event on the top line of the puzzle piece, and write a sentence describing the event below it.
2. Use markers or colored pencils to draw a picture in the white space.
3. When you're done, cut out each of the pieces.
4. Place the pieces in sequential order so that the earliest date is on the left. Tape them together from the back.

A Letter From the Second Continental Congress

Write a letter to George Washington urging him to accept the nomination as Commander-in-Chief of the Continental Army. Write from the point of view of John Adams while he was attending the Second Continental Congress. Use the brainstorming graphic organizers below to organize your thoughts.

Reasons why the Second Continental Congress met

Reasons why Washington would be the best Commander-in-Chief

Information about the Continental Army

Remember, your "business letter" should include:

- [ ] the proper form for the heading, salutation, body, closing, and signature
- [ ] a date reflecting the time when it was written
- [ ] three complete, detailed paragraphs
- [ ] information related to the topics in the brainstorming graphic organizers
- [ ] correct grammar and spelling
- [ ] an envelope, addressed to Washington's home in Mount Vernon, Virginia
- [ ] a creative postage stamp with a postmark from Philadelphia

Directions

1. Fold panel 5 so that its right edge meets the line that separates panels 3 and 4.

2. Fold panel 3 to the right so that its left edge meets the right edge of panel 2.

Creating the Panels

Panel 1: This will be the cover of your guide. Include a title, your name, and a picture that illustrates the Battle of Bunker Hill. Be creative and detailed.

Panel 2: Use the graph on panel 3 to answer these questions. Use scratch paper if necessary.

Panels 4 and 5: Write a detailed and thoughtful essay about the Battle of Bunker Hill. First write a rough draft on another piece of paper and then transfer it to the panels. Your essay should answer the following questions:

1. Why was Bunker Hill considered a strategic location?

2. How many battles were fought and what were the results of those battles?

3. Why do you think General Israel Putnam said, "Don't fire until you see the whites of their eyes"?

4. What was the significance of the Battle of Bunker Hill?

Panel 1

Panel 6

1. About how many soldiers fought in the Battle of Bunker Hill in total?

2. How many more soldiers did the Americans have than the British?

3. How many Americans were killed or wounded?

4. How many British soldiers were killed or wounded?

5. What percentage of the British soldiers were killed or wounded?

6. How many Americans survived the Battle of Bunker Hill?

Panel 2

Essay

Essay

The Battle of Bunker Hill

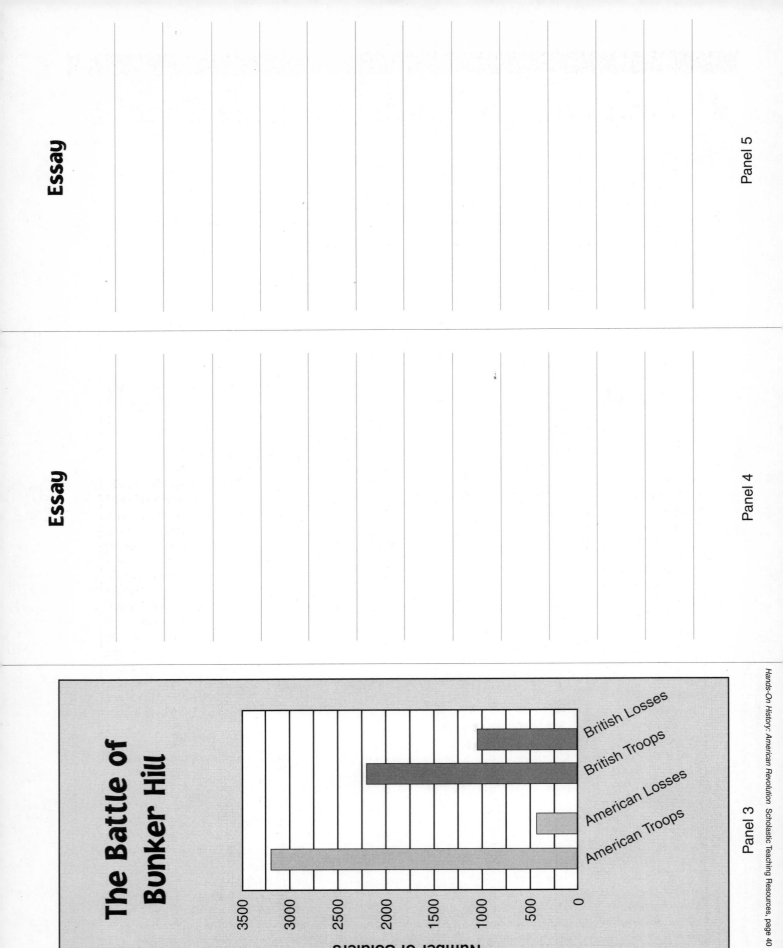

Number of Soldiers

3500 · 3000 · 2500 · 2000 · 1500 · 1000 · 500 · 0

British Losses
British Troops
American Losses
American Troops

Hands-On History: American Revolution Scholastic Teaching Resources, page 40

1. Cut out the large box below.
2. Poke a hole in the center dot and cut along the solid lines.
3. Fold the panels along the dotted lines.
4. Glue the perimeter of the box onto a piece of blank paper.
5. Lift up the flaps and answer the questions on the paper behind each panel.

CONGRESS, JULY 4, 1776.

Declar

Hm

rse of human ev
earth, the separ
leclare the caus
tor with certain
riving their jus
r to abolish it,
ffect their Safe
ly all experienc
istomed. But w
t, it is their du
now the neces
s and usurpatio
    He has ref
nportance, unle
refused to pass
  inestimable to
of their public
osing with man
ereby the Legi
ngers of invasi
s for Naturaliza
e has obstructe
the tenure of th
our people, ana
cted to render

al bands which
s God entitle th
uths to be self-
ursuit of Happin
m of Government
principles and o
nts long establi
ls are sufferabl
he same Object,
their future seci
nment. The hi
yranny over the
public good.
ed; and when s
nless those peo
ther legislative
with his measur
le has refused
eople at large f
ndeavoured to p
grations hither,
for establishin
  He has erecte
s of peace, Sta
  He has con

1. Which delegate was chosen to write the Declaration of Independence?

2. On what date did the Congress adopt the Declaration of Independence?

3. Who was the first person to sign the Declaration of Independence? Why did he write his name so large?

4. What unalienable rights does the Declaration say people have?

r, and unacknowledged by our laws; giving his Assent to their Acts of pretended Legislation:
m, by a mock Trial, from punishment for any Murders which they should commit on the Inhabita
For imposing Taxes on us without our Consent: For depriving us in many cases, of the benefi
ded offences: For abolishing the free System of English Laws in a neighbouring Province, es
so as to render it at once an example and fit instrument for introducing the same absolute rule
luable Laws, and altering fundamentally the Forms of our Governments: For suspending our c

Declaration of Independence Quiz Panel 2

1. Cut out the large box below.
2. Poke a hole in the center dot and cut along the solid lines.
3. Fold the panels along the dotted lines.
4. Glue the perimeter of the box onto a piece of blank paper.
5. Lift up the flaps and answer the questions on the paper behind each panel.

in the Legislature, a right inestimable to them and formidable to tyrants only.   He has
distant from the depository of their public Records, for the sole purpose of fatiguing them into c
Houses repeatedly, for opposing with manly firmness his invasions on the rights of the people.
se others to be elected; whereby the Legislative powers, incapable of Annihilation, have return
intime exposed to all the dangers of invasion from without, and convulsions within.

5. What did Benjamin Franklin mean when he said, "Gentlemen, we must all hang together or else we shall all hang separately?"

6. What is one of the most important differences between a democratic republic and the British government at the time of the American Revolution?

BRITISH

AMERICANS

MILITARY ADVANTAGES

Fold up here.

BRITISH

AMERICANS

MILITARY DISADVANTAGES

Fold up here.

American Revolution Circlebook

After writing the paragraph and drawing the picture, fold the page along the dotted line. Reopen the page and cut out the circle.

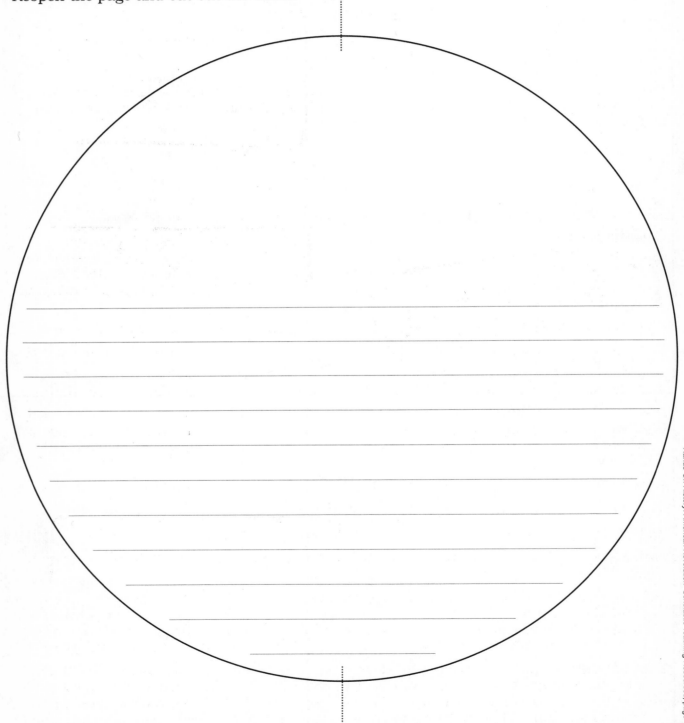

The Boston Tea Party

by Sarah J. Glasscock

Cast of Characters
(in order of appearance)

Women 1 and 2
Men 1–3
Sam Adams: a Patriot
John Hancock: a Patriot and merchant
Francis Rotch: Captain of the *Dartmouth*

British Officer
Honor Turner: a Boston woman
Elizabeth Harrison: a Boston woman
Thomas Boylston: a Boston merchant

Act 1

Scene 1: The night of December 16, 1773. Old South Church in Boston.

NARRATOR: Old South Church is filled with people. It's also filled with tension and excitement. Everyone is talking. Three ships—the *Dartmouth*, *Eleanor*, and *Beaver*—are anchored in Boston Harbor. The ships are filled with 90,000 pounds of tea, but the people of Boston won't take the tea. And the British won't let the ships leave and go to another port. Why? Listen—

WOMAN 1: I don't mind paying a bit of tax on my tea. It's the rest of it that I don't like.

WOMAN 2: I don't mind it at all. Only one company can bring in the tea, and they get to choose who sells it to us. So what? It's still tea, isn't it?

MAN 1: First it's tea—then what? They'll be putting a tax on going to church or talking to your friends on the street.

MAN 2: The British won't let Francis Rotch take the *Dartmouth* out of the harbor and sail her to another port. Francis doesn't want any trouble. He's willing to take his cargo somewhere else.

MAN 3: The British don't want any trouble. They'll let him leave. You'll see.

MAN 1: If they don't, we have a little surprise for them.

MAN 3 *(looking suspiciously at Man 1)*: What do you mean?

WOMAN 1: Sshh! *(nudging Man 1)* There's Mr. Rotch now! Look at him! Going right up to Sam Adams.

NARRATOR: The crowd inside the church is silent. Will the British let the three ships, still loaded with tea, sail out of Boston Harbor? They watch as Francis Rotch tells Sam Adams and John Hancock about his meeting with the British. Rotch shakes his head each time Sam Adams asks him a question. A low murmur starts in the audience.

SAM ADAMS *(standing up)*: People of Boston! Friends! The British will not let Mr. Rotch take the *Dartmouth*—his own ship—out of Boston Harbor. They insist that we must take the tea. I'm sorry—they insist that we must buy the tea from their agents, and their agents only. They insist we must pay a tax on this tea. They insist that we are not free to decide these things. *(He pauses and then shakes his head.)* Ladies and gentlemen—this meeting can do nothing more to save the country.

MAN 1 *(springing up)*: They want us to take the tea? Then let's take it! We'll turn Boston Harbor into a teapot!

WOMAN 1: Aye, we'll hold a tea party the British won't ever forget!

MAN 2: To the *Dartmouth*! We'll free your ship, Mr. Rotch!

JOHN HANCOCK: Let every man do what is right in his own eyes!

NARRATOR: Shouting and talking excitedly, the people pour out of the church and head for Griffin's Wharf where the three ships are anchored.

Scene 2: Later   night at Griffin's Wharf in Boston Harbor where the
Dartmouth, Eleanor, **and** *Beaver* **are anchored.**

NARRATOR: Three groups of men and boys carrying torches board the ships. Some have stopped long enough to darken their faces with ash and paint so they look like Indians. No one says a word. They know that there's no turning back.

JOHN HANCOCK *(approaching the captain of the* Dartmouth*)*: We won't harm you or your ship, sir. All we ask is that you stand aside.

CAPTAIN FRANCIS ROTCH: I don't have a choice, do I?

JOHN HANCOCK: No. And neither do we. The British have decided for us.

NARRATOR: The Boston men work quickly. They bring up the chests of tea and dump the contents into the harbor. When all the chests are empty, the men sweep the decks of the ships. The people of Boston want to send a message to the British: They demand freedom and liberty, and will fight for it. But they believe in law and order, too.

Act 2

Scene 1: May 10, 1774. Griffin's Wharf.

NARRATOR: The tea party in Boston angers King George III and the British. A new set of acts, or rules, is forced upon the people of Boston. At Griffin's Wharf, a crowd gathers to read the list of rules.

MAN 1: They can't do this!

WOMAN 1: We knew there'd be a price to pay for dumping the tea.

MAN 1: But this! This is intolerable! Closing the port of Boston until we pay for the tea! Moving the capital from here to Salem! Forbidding town meetings! Making us feed British soldiers and put them up in our homes!

WOMAN 1: They mean to starve us. They mean to close down our shops. If they close the harbor, no boats can come in or go out.

MAN 2: You've left out the worst one. They've taken away the colonial assembly from us. From now on, the governor chooses the members of the assembly. And who chooses the royal governor? Not us! We've lost our right to vote on the members. We've lost our voice.

WOMAN 2: A fine fix you've got us into. Dressing up like Indians and ruining perfectly good tea. Why pick a fight with England? We'll lose, and then what?

WOMAN 1: Can't you read, woman? They're taking away our rights! They're treating us like children. They want us to be good and keep quiet.

MAN 1: Aye, as long as we send them boats loaded with timber and fish and fur! They need us, our resources, more than we need them!

MAN 3 (*pointing to Woman 2*): No, she's right. We've got friends in England. The colonies *will* get representatives in Parliament if we go slowly. No more taxation without representation. The colonies *will* have a voice in England. We'll have a say in how we're governed—

WOMAN 1: It's too late for that. He's right (*nods to Man 1 and then taps the list of rules*); these are intolerable. They're intolerable acts.

WOMAN 2: Don't say I didn't warn you. When you're on your knees, begging the British to forgive you, and they're not interested. Just don't say I didn't warn you.

(*A group of British soldiers marches toward the crowd.*)

BRITISH OFFICER: Move on, move on! You've had time enough to read. If it was up to me, I'd have you fish every single tea leaf out of the harbor. Move on, I said! Come on!

MAN 2 (*muttering*): If it was up to me, I'd stuff every single leaf of tea down your throat— all ninety thousand pounds of it.

BRITISH OFFICER: What's that!?

WOMAN 2: Nothing! He was just telling me to keep quiet and mind my own business.

(*The crowd moves off together.*)

Scene 2: Later in 1774. The warehouses along Griffin's Wharf.

NARRATOR: The British close Boston Harbor. Large amounts of coffee and sugar sit in some Boston warehouses. These goods arrived before the harbor was shut down. The owners of these warehouses are now charging high prices for the products. They think the people of Boston will have no choice but to pay the prices. The women of Boston disagree. One morning, they take matters into their own hands. A group of at least a hundred women march down to Thomas Boylston's warehouse. They're wheeling a large cart and smaller hand trucks.

JOHN HANCOCK (*He hears the noise and comes out of his office nearby.*): Ladies! What's happening? Where are you going?

HONOR TURNER (*answering without stopping*): To Boylston's, for some coffee.

JOHN HANCOCK (*falling in step with Honor*): But he's charging an arm and leg—

HONOR TURNER: Oh, I think he'll come down on his price for us.

(*The women stop in front of Boylston's warehouse.*)

ELIZABETH HARRISON: Mr. Boylston! Mr. Thomas Boylston!

HONOR TURNER: We've come for your coffee!

THOMAS BOYLSTON (*He comes out of the warehouse and locks the door behind him.*): Ladies! Good morning, good morning! One at a time, one at a time! Plenty of coffee! Price has gone up a bit, you know. Six shillings a pound.

ELIZABETH HARRISON: Your keys, please, Mr. Boylston. We've come for your coffee.

THOMAS BOYLSTON (*laughing and thinking she's joking*): Now, now, ladies. I'm a merchant. I must make my living. How will I feed my family if I give away my coffee?

HONOR TURNER: Six shillings for a pound of coffee! Shame on you! You're taking the food out of our children's mouths.

THOMAS BOYLSTON *(starting to realize the women are serious)*: I didn't throw any tea overboard, ladies. If your children are hungry, it's your husbands' fault, not mine.

ELIZABETH HARRISON: *(Elizabeth and others block his way.)* You're a greedy man, Mr. Boylston. It's money you love, not freedom, liberty, or your family.

THOMAS BOYLSTON *(coldly)*: You are free *not* to buy my coffee.

HONOR TURNER: We have not come here to buy your coffee, sir. We have come here to take it. Now, hand over the keys to the warehouse, and we'll be quick about it.

THOMAS BOYLSTON: I will not!

(Elizabeth Harrison grabs Boylston by the neck and tosses him into the cart. Boylston looks around in a panic. Then as a group of women surround him, he sees John Hancock in the crowd.)

THOMAS BOYLSTON: Hancock! John Hancock! Help me!

JOHN HANCOCK: Oh, I would give up the keys if I were you, sir.

HONOR TURNER: We would like you to hand over the keys, Mr. Boylston. But if you will not, then we will take them from you.

THOMAS BOYLSTON: All right! All right! *(He tosses the keys to the ground.)* There! Go ahead and steal my coffee! You're no better than King George!

NARRATOR: Honor unlocks the warehouse. The women dump Boylston out of the cart. Then they wheel the empty cart into the warehouse. They work as quietly as the men on board the three ships did. In a few minutes, they emerge with the cart loaded with coffee. Elizabeth Harrison stops beside Boylston who's still sitting on the ground.

ELIZABETH HARRISON: You're the one pretending to be king, Mr. Boylston. Charging such high prices. Expecting us to make you a rich man.

THOMAS BOYLSTON *(shouting)*: I hope my coffee keeps you awake all night long! You'll have plenty to think about and be sorry for! *(muttering to himself)* A man can't even try to make a good living for himself and his family. *(appealing to Hancock)* You're a rich man. You know what I'm talking about. I haven't done anything wrong.

JOHN HANCOCK *(approaching and holding out his hand to help Boylston stand up)*: The women of Boston seem to think you have done something wrong.

HONOR TURNER *(holding out the keys)*: Your keys, Mr. Boylston. It was a pleasure doing business with you.

(Boylston ignores Hancock's outstretched hand. As the women leave, he's left behind, sitting on the ground.)

NARRATOR: The name for the harsh British rules stuck. But the Intolerable Acts backfired on the British. The acts united the American colonies. Food and supplies flowed into Boston. Virginia called for a Continental Congress. Representatives from every colony met in Philadelphia in the fall of 1774 to talk about what was happening in Boston. Committees of correspondence sprang up. The committees of each colony reported about British actions in its area and how its colonists were responding. Alarmed, the British sent more troops to Boston. A year later, the first shots in the American Revolution were fired.